Texas Bible English
Level 1
Student Book

For video instructions for each lesson, go to:

www.texasbibleenglish.com

Texas Bible English
Level 1
Student Book

By: Julie Davis
Illustrated By: Chloe Mooring

Table of Contents

Color codes for vowel sounds:

Blue vowels say short sounds:

a apple
e elephant
i iguana
o octopus
u umbrella

Red vowels say long sounds:

a ape
e eagle
i I
o open
u use

Other color codes:

Purple for silent letters
Green "s" added to words

Color codes for verbs:

Orange root verb present tense
Brown past tense
Gray future tense

Lesson 1

Adam and Eve	

1	

		a a-e

NOUNS: Person, Place, Thing (Who? Or What?)

a	a	a-e
_____	_____	_____
_____	_____	_____
_____	an	_____
_____	and	_____
_____		

1. _____   _____   the _____

2. _____   _____   _____

3. _____   _____   _____

4. _____   _____   the _____

5. _____   _____

1

2

3

4

5

-an	-ad	-ake	-ame	-ade
m	f	sn	n	m
c	m	f	s	sp
r	r	r	f	tr
t	t	t	c	f

"In the beginning, <u>God</u> <u>created</u> (<u>made</u>) the heavens and the <u>earth</u>." Genesis 1:1 HCSB

the

Lesson 2

Noah's Ark

1	
2	

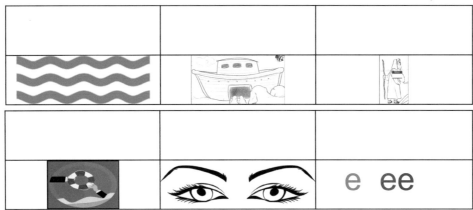

e ee

NOUNS: Person, Place, Thing (Who? Or What?)

e	ee	1 one	2 two
	Hello my name is		
10			
	the		

1. _____ _____ the _____

2. _____ _____ _____

3. _____ _____ the _____

4. _____ _____ the _____

5. _____ _____ are on the _____
2 _____

6. _____ _____ the _____ _____

7. _____ _____ are on the _____

2

8. _____ _____ are on the _____

2

9. _____ is on the _____

10. _____ _____ _____

1
2
3
4
5

-en	-ed	-e	-eet	-eat
f	f	w	m	m
m	m	b	str	s
d	r	m	f	tr
t	l	sh	gr	b

"<u>God</u> remembered <u>Noah</u>, all those alive, and all the <u>animals</u> with him in the <u>ark</u>. <u>God</u> sent a wind over the <u>earth</u> so that the <u>waters</u> receded." Genesis 8:1

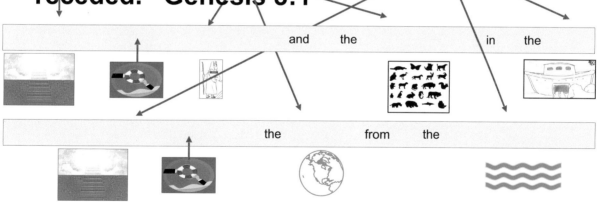

Lesson 3

Father Abraham

Hello Hi

1
2
3

Abraham
Isaac
Sarah

	i i-e	

NOUNS: Person, Place, Thing (Who? Or What?)

i	i-e	1	2, 3, 4

1. _____ ↓ is the _____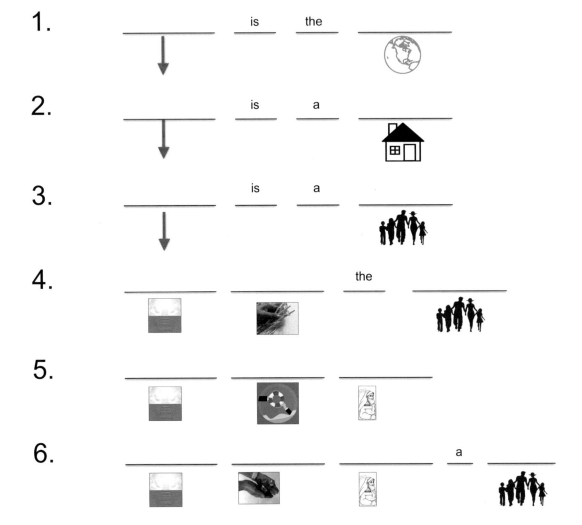

2. _____ ↓ is a _____

3. _____ ↓ is a _____

4. _____ _____ the _____

5. _____ _____ _____

6. _____ _____ _____ a _____

7.

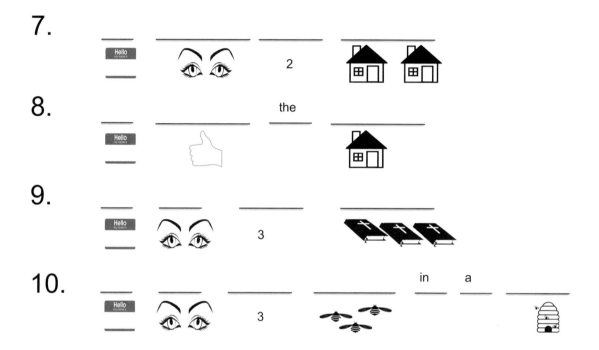

8. the

9.

10. in a

1	
2	
3	
4	
5	

-in	-id	-ike	-ime	-ild
m	m	p	d	ch
f	l	b	l	m
t	r	l	sl	w
s	b	h	t	

"I (<u>God</u>) will bless her (Sarah), and indeed I will give (<u>gave</u>) you (<u>Abraham</u>) <u>a</u> son by her(<u>family</u>)." Genesis 17:16

Lesson 4 | Joseph's Coat of Colors | Good Morning

1	
2	
3	
4	

NOUNS: Person, Place, Thing (Who? Or What?)

o	o-e	1	2, 3, 4…

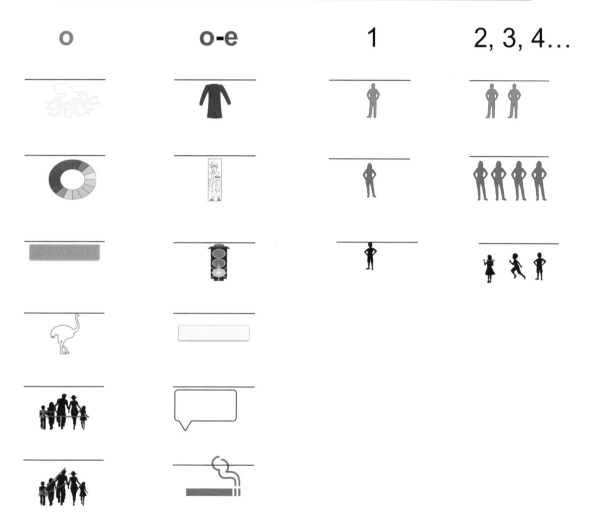

1. _____ _____ the _____ _____

2. _____ _____ _____

3. _____ _____ _____ a _____ of _____

4. _____ _____ is _____

5. _____ _____ is the _____ in the _____

6. _____ _____ is the _____ in the _____

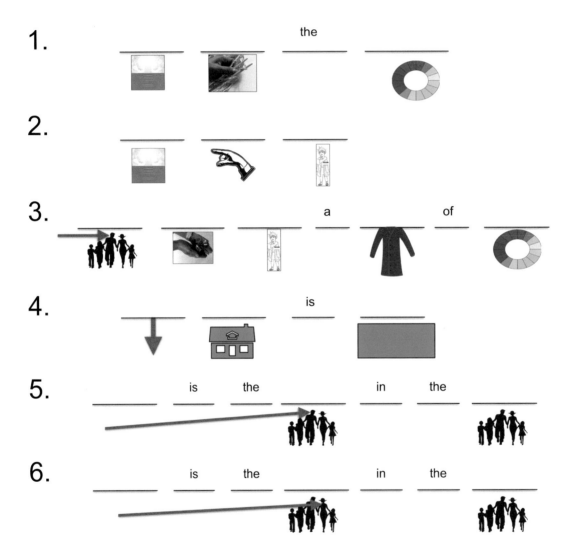

7. _____ is a _____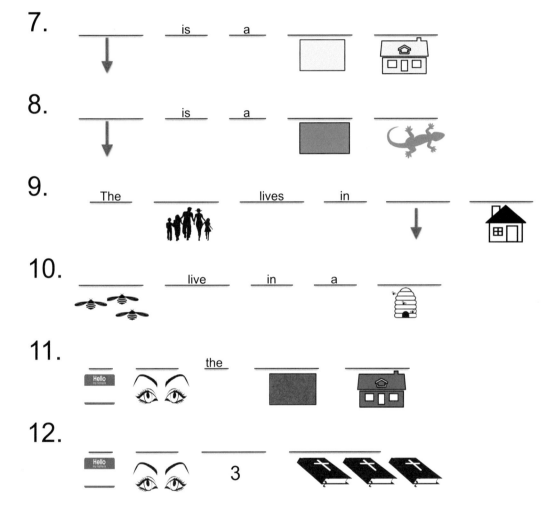

8. _____ is a _____

9. The _____ lives in _____

10. _____ live in a _____

11. _____ the _____

12. _____ 3 _____

33

1	
2	
3	
4	
5	

-on	-od	-oke	-ome	-old
m	m	p	d	c
c	l	sm	R	m
p	r	j	h	f
s	b	w		g

"<u>God</u> <u>sent</u> me <u>(Joseph)</u> before you(<u>family</u>) to preserve for you a remnant in the earth, and <u>to</u> keep you alive(<u>save</u>)…" Genesis 45:7 HCSB

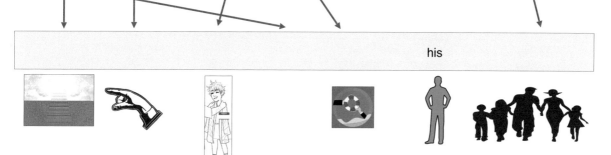

his

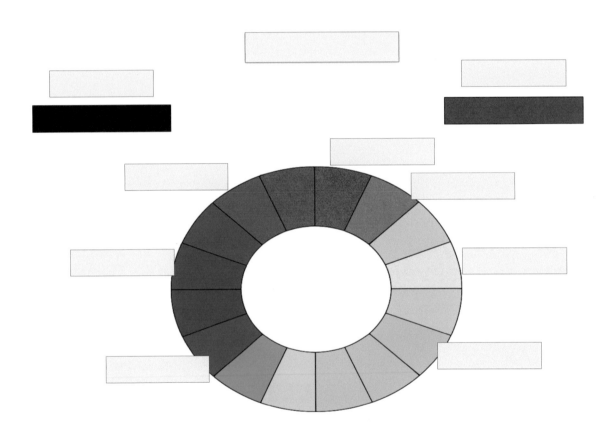

Lesson 5 | The Burning Bush | Good afternoon

Moses

1
2
3
4
5

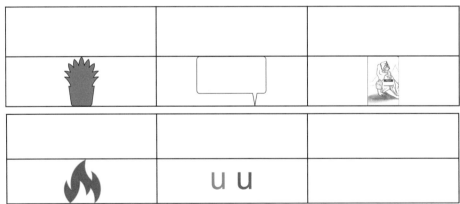

	u u	

NOUNS: Person, Place, Thing (Who? Or What?)

u	u	1	2,3,4…

1. _____ _____ the _____
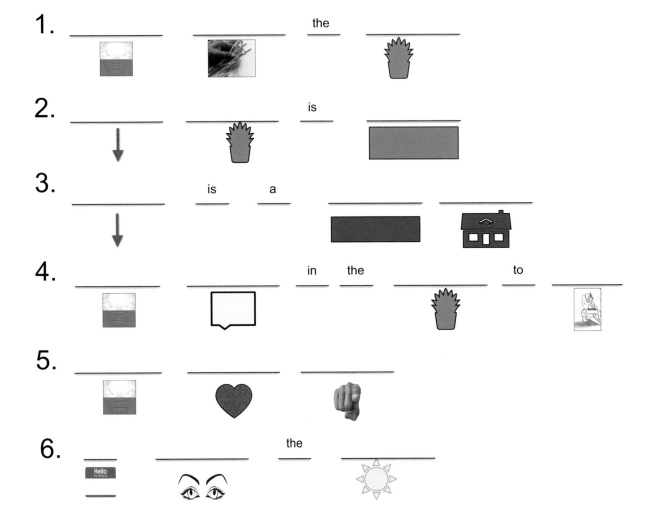

2. _____ _____ is _____

3. _____ is a _____ _____

4. _____ _____ in the _____ to _____

5. _____ _____ _____

6. ___ _____ the _____

7. _____ _____ _____ _____ to _____

8. _____ _____ the _____ _____

9. _____ _____ the _____ _____
   2

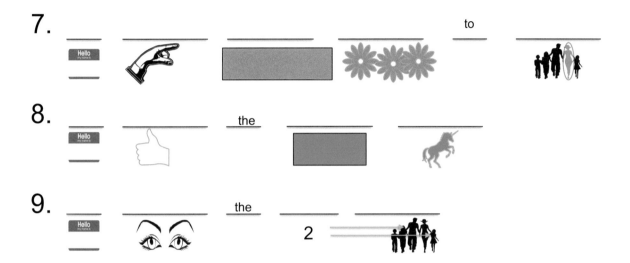

1	
2	
3	
4	
5	

-ur	-ud	-uke	-ue	-ew(u)
p	m	L	bl	ch
f	s	D	tr	n
b	b	j	S	bl
s	c	p	d	d

"<u>God</u> <u>called out(spoke)</u> to him (<u>Moses</u>) <u>from</u> the <u>bush</u>, 'Moses, Moses.'"
Exodus 3:4(end) HCSB

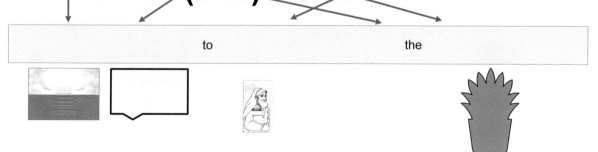

to   the

44

Lesson 6 | God parts the Sea | Good evening.

Moses

1
2
3
4
5
6

👥 👥👥	🚶	▪
🖼	Rr, Ss	

NOUNS: Person, Place, Thing (Who? Or What?)

r-	**r-**	**S-**	**S-**

1. _____ _____ the _____

2. _____ _____ _____

3. The _____ is _____

4. _____ _____ _____ and the _____

5. _____ _____ the _____

6. _____ _____ to _____ in the _____

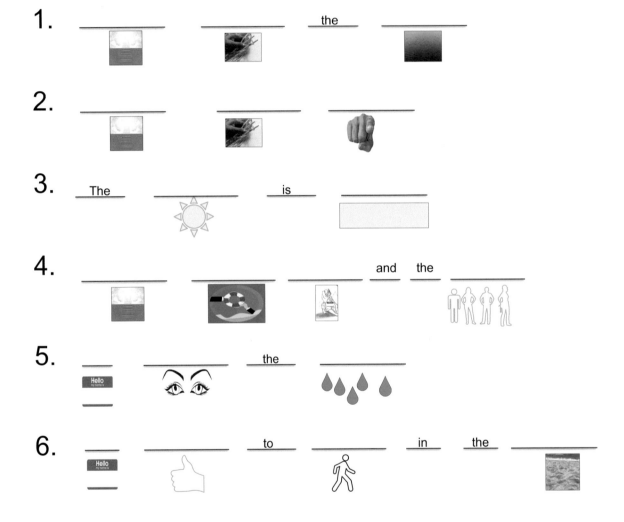

48

7. _____ is a _____ _____

8. _____ _____ the _____ to the _____

9. _____ _____ to the _____

10. _____ _____ the _____ 6 _____

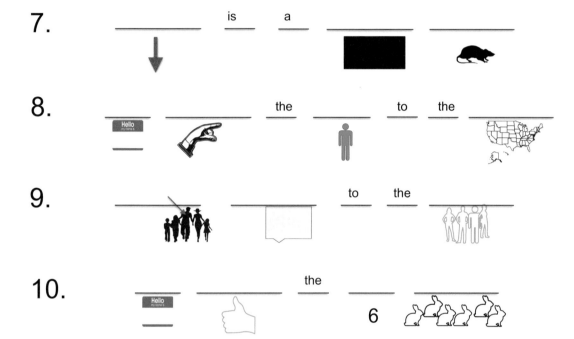

49

r	a	_ _ck	_ _d	_ _m
r	e	_ _st	_ _p	_ _ady
r	i	_ _p	_ _b	_ _g
r	o	_ _b	_ _d	_ _t
r	u	_ _b	_ _st	_ _n

r	a	_ _id	_ _in	_ _te
r	e	_ _al	_ _ad	_ _ap
r	i	_ _pe	_ _de	_ _se
r	o	_ _pe	_ _ad	_ _de
r	u	_ _de	_ _le	_ _e

s	a	_ _t	_ _ck	_ _p
s	e	_ _t	_ _ll	_ _lf
s	i	_ _p	_ _ck	_ _lk
s	o	_ _ck	_ _d	_ _me
s	u	_ _ck	_ _m	_ _lk

s	a	_ _me	_ _ke	_ _le
s	e	_ _ek	_ _em	_ _ed
s	i	_ _de	_ _te	_ _gn
s	o	_ _ak	_ _	_ _da
s	u	_o_p	_ _e	

"...and the <u>Lord(God)</u> <u>drove (sent) the sea back</u> with a powerful east wind all that night and turned the sea into dry land. So the waters were <u>divided(to the sides)</u> and Israel (<u>people</u>) <u>went(walked)</u> through the sea on dry ground." Exodus 14:21 HCSB

The

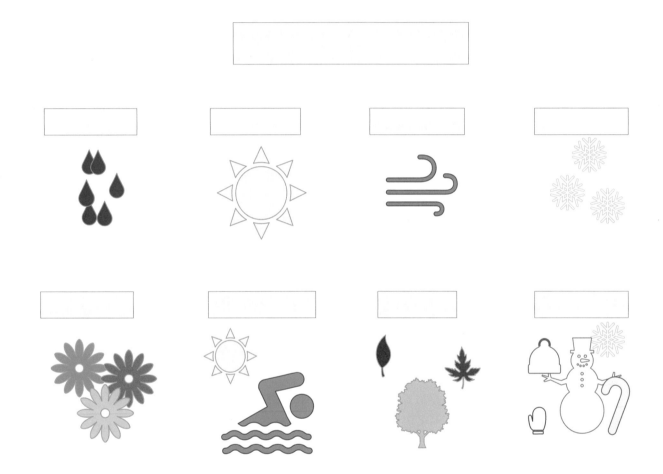

Lesson 7 | The Walls of Jericho

Joshua

Good night.

1
2
3
4
5
6
7

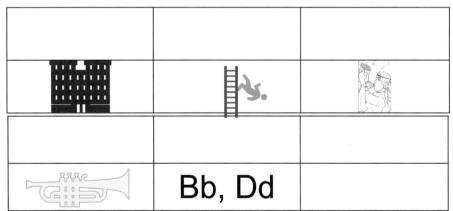

	Bb, Dd	

NOUNS: Person, Place, Thing (Who? Or What?)

b-	b-	d-	d-

1. _____ _____ the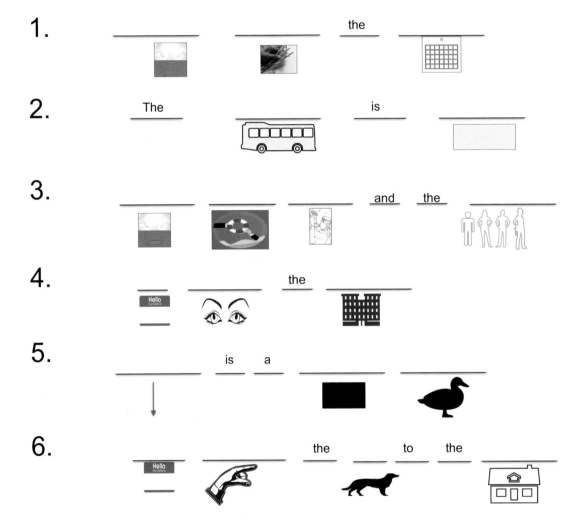

2. The _____ is _____

3. _____ _____ and the _____

4. _____ the _____

5. _____ is a _____ _____

6. _____ _____ the _____ to the _____

7. The _____ _____ _____ to the _____

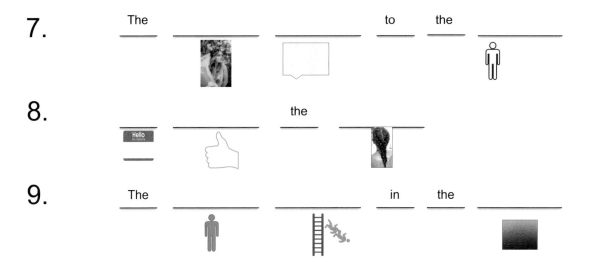

8. _____ _____ the _____ _____

9. The _____ _____ in the _____

b	a	_ _t	_ _d	_ _ck
b	e	_ _d	_ _nt	_ _t
b	i	_ _g	_ _b	_ _n
b	o	_ _ss	_ _mb	_ _n
b	u	_ _n	_ _t	_ _s

b	a	_ _it	_ r_in	_ r_id
b	e	_ _e	_ l_ed	_ _et
b	i	_ _te	_ r_de	_ r_te
b	o	_ _at	_ _th	_ _ne
b	u	_ l_e		

d	a	_ _d	_ _m	_ _b
d	e	_ _sk	_ _nt	_ _bt
d	i	_ _g	_ _n	_ _d
d	o	_ _g	_ _t	_ _ck
d	u	_ _ck	_._mp	_ _d

d	a	_ _te	_ _y	_ r_in
d	e	_ _ed	_ _ep	_ r_am
d	i	_ _me	_ _e	_ r_ve
d	o	_ _ze	_ _me	_ r_ne
d	u	_ _ne	_ _de	_ _ke

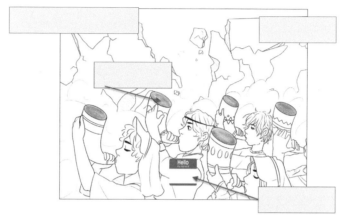

"...<u>the</u> <u>people</u> <u>shouted</u>(<u>yelled</u>) with a great shout and <u>the</u> <u>wall</u> <u>fell</u> <u>down</u> flat..." Joshua 6:20 HCSB

1	2	3	4	5	6	7
8	9	10	11	12	13	14
15	16	17	18	19	20	21
22	23	24	25	26	27	28
29	30	31				

Review Questions

Lesson 1:

1. What did God make?

2. Who did God make first?

3. Did God make you?

Lesson 2:

1. What was on all the earth?

2. Who did God save on the ark?

Review Questions

Lesson 3:

1. What did God give to Abraham?

2. Where does a family live?

3. Who is in your family?

Lesson 4:

1. What did God send Joseph to do?

2. Who gave Joseph a coat of colors?

3. What did God give you?

Review Questions

Lesson 5:

1. How did God speak to Moses?

2. How does God speak to us?

3. How do you speak to God?

Lesson 6:

1. How did God save the people?

2. How does God save us?

Lesson 7:

1. What did the walls do?

Lesson 8 | David and Goliath

1	
2	
3	
4	
5	
6	
7	
8	

		Mm, Nn

NOUNS: Person, Place, Thing (Who? Or What?)

m-	m-	n-	n-

1. _____ _____ the _____
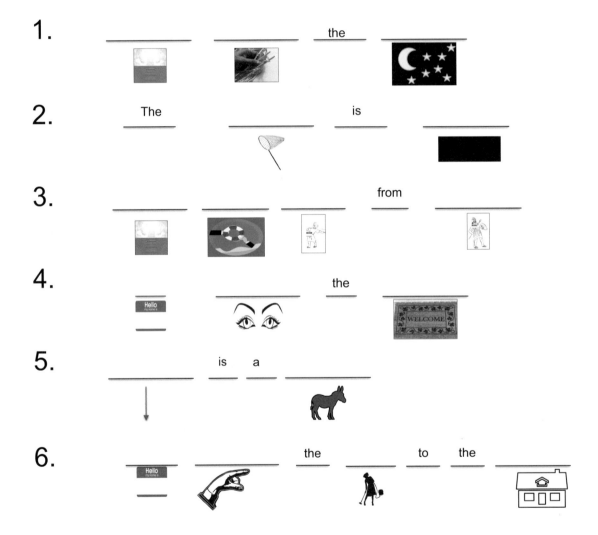

2. The _____ _____ is _____

3. _____ _____ _____ from _____

4. _____ _____ the _____

5. _____ is a _____

6. _____ _____ the _____ to the _____

68

7. _____ _____ to the _____ _____

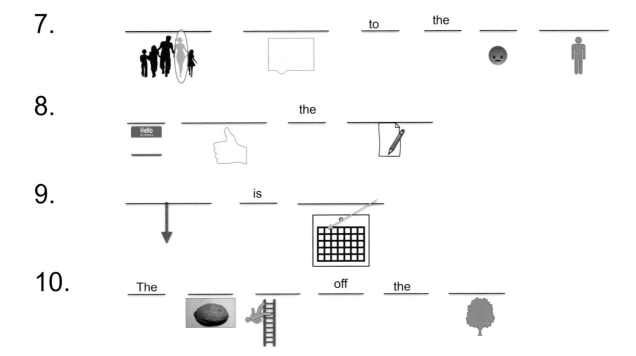

8. _____ _____ the _____

9. _____ is _____

10. The _____ off the _____

1	
2	
3	
4	
5	
6	
7	
8	
9	
10	
11	
12	

m	a	_ _t	_ _d	m_n
m	e	_ _d	_ _ss	m_n
m	i	_ _t	_ _x	m_n
m	o	_ _n	_ _m	m_p
m	u	_ _d	_ _t	m_g

m	a	_ _id	_ _de	_ _ke
m	e	_ _et	_ _	_ _al
m	i	_ _le	_ _ne	
m	o	_ _le	_ses	_ _de
m	u	_ _sic	_ _le	_ _te

n	a	_ _p	g_ _t	kn_ck
n	e	_ _ck	_ _st	n_t
n	i	k_ _t	_ _p	
n	o	_ _t	_ _d	kn_b
n	u	_ _t	_ _mb	n_mber

n	a	_ _me	_ _il	
n	e	_ _at	_ _ed	k_ _el
n	i	_ _ne	_ _ght	_ _le
n	o	_ _se	_ _	_ _te
n	u	_ _de		

"**David**… took out a stone, slung it, and hit the Philistine (**Goliath**) on his forehead… he struck down the Philistine (Goliath) and **killed** him."
1 Samuel 17:49-50 HCSB

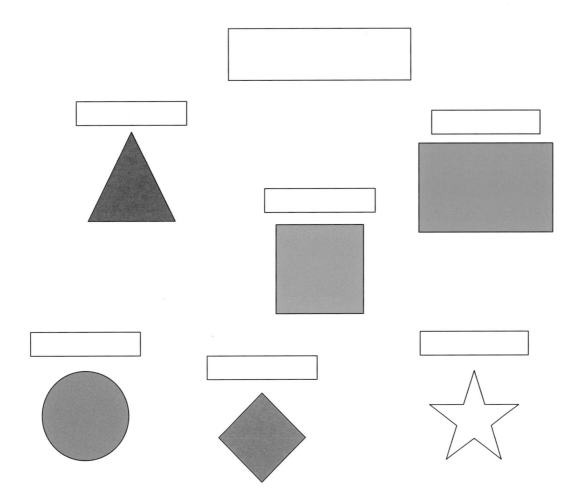

Lesson 9

King Solomon

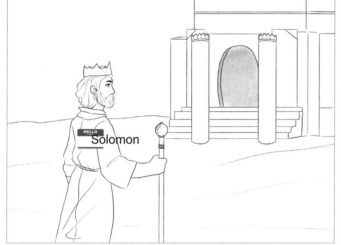

	Thank you.
1	
2	
3	
4	
5	
6	
7	
8	
9	

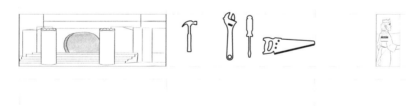

 ♪ 𝄞 ♫ **Ll, Tt**

NOUNS: Person, Place, Thing (Who? Or What What?)

l-	l-	t-	t-

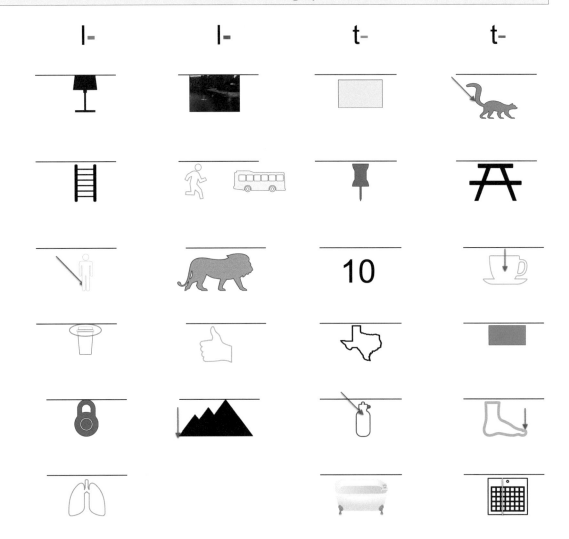

1. _____ _____ the _____
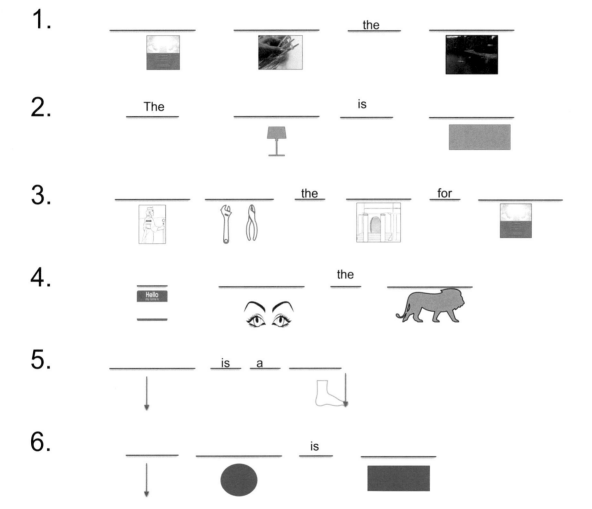

2. The _____ is _____

3. _____ _____ the _____ for _____

4. _____ _____ the _____

5. _____ is a _____

6. _____ _____ is _____

77

7. _____ _____ _____ to the _____
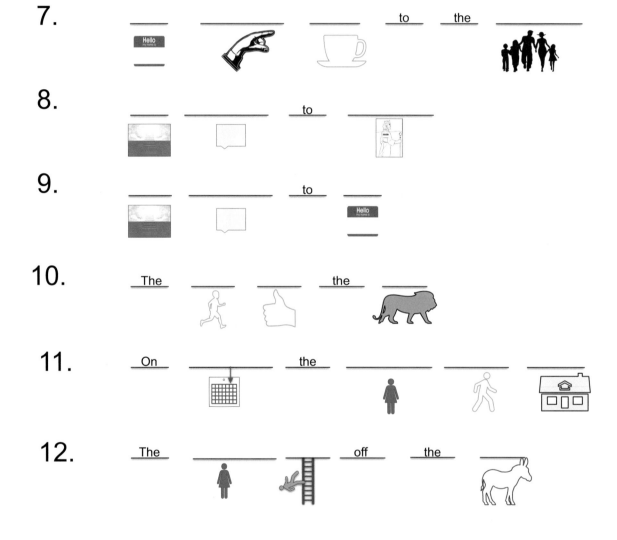

8. _____ _____ to _____

9. _____ _____ to _____

10. The _____ _____ the _____

11. On _____ the _____ _____ _____

12. The _____ _____ off the _____

78

1	
2	
3	
4	
5	
6	
7	
8	
9	
10	
11	
12	

l	a	_ _ke	_ _te	_ _me
l	e	_ _ak	_ _an	_ _ad
l	i	_ _on	_ _ke	_ _ght
l	o	_ _be	_ _an	_ _w
l	u	_ _ke	_ _be	

l	a	_ _mp	_ _dder	_ _nd
l	e	_ _g	_ _ss	_ _t
l	i	_ _d	_ _ck	_ _mp
l	o	_ _g	_ _st	_ _ng
L	u	_ _ng	_ _ck	_ _g

t	a	_ _n	_ _ck	_ _x
t	e	_ _n	_ _xas	_ _ll
t	i	_ _ll	_ _p	_ _m
t	o	_ _p	_ _ck	_ _t
t	u	_ _b	_ _g	_ _ck

t	a	_ _il	_ _me	_ _ke
t	e	_ _a	_ _al	_ _am
t	i	_ _me	_ _de	_ _ght
t	o	_ _e	_ _ast	_ _te
t	u	_ _be	_ _esday	_ _ne

"And the word (<u>spoke to</u>) of <u>the Lord(God)</u> came to <u>Solomon</u>… So <u>Solomon built</u> the house (<u>Temple</u>)…'"
1 Kings 6:11,14 KJV

the

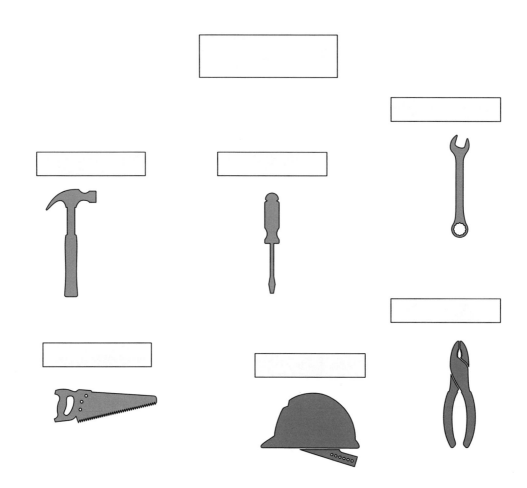

Lesson 10 | Friends in the Fire | You're welcome.

1
2
3
4
5
6
7
8
9
10

		Hh, Pp

NOUNS: Person, Place, Thing (Who? Or What?)

h-	h-	p-	p-

1. ____ ____ the ____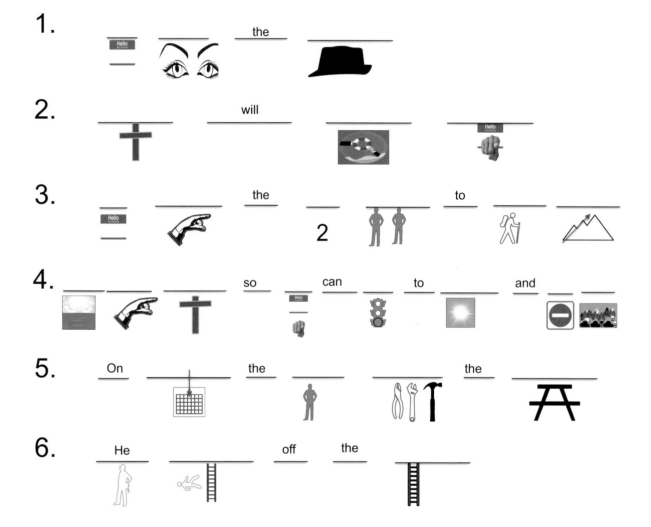

2. ____ will ____ ____

3. ____ ____ the 2 ____ to ____ ____

4. ____ ____ ____ so ____ can ____ to ____ and ____

5. On ____ the ____ ____ the ____

6. He ____ ____ off ____ the ____

86

7. The _____ _____ _____ _____
8. The _____ was _____ The _____ _____ _____
9. The _____ _____ the _____ into the _____
10. _____ _____ His _____ to the _____
11. _____ _____ the _____ _____
12. The _____ did _____ _____ in the _____

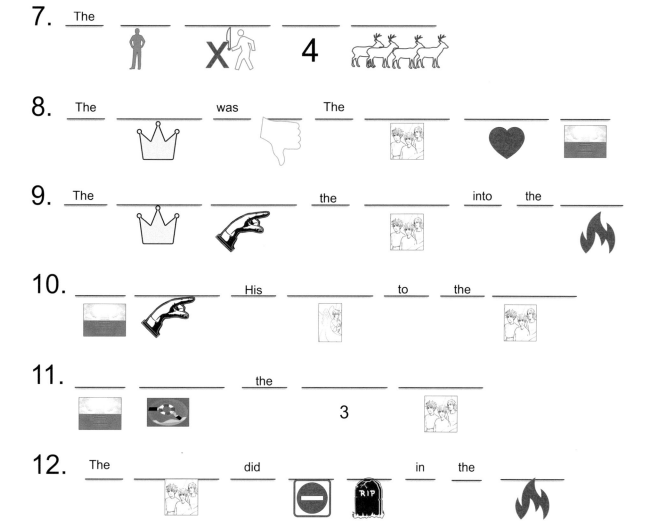

1	
2	
3	
4	
5	
6	
7	
8	
9	
10	
11	
12	

h	a	_ _t	_ _nd	_ _s
h	e	_ _ad	_ _ll	_ _lp
h	i	_ _t	_ _m	_ _s
h	o	_ _t	_ _p	_ _g
h	u	_ _g	_ _t	_ _nt

h	a	_ _il	_ _te	_ _y
h	e	_ _	_ _at	_ _el
h	i	_ _	_ _ke	_ _gh
h	o	_ _me	_ _le	_ _pe
h	u	_ _e	(j) _ _ge	_ _man

p	a	_ _n	_ _ddle	_ _t
p	e	_ _n	_ _t	_ _st
p	i	_ _g	_ _ll	_ _ck
p	o	_ _t	_ _p	_ _d
p	u	_ _g	_ _n	_ _nt

p	a	_ _il	_ _int	_ _y
p	e	_ _a	_ _al	_ _ek
p	i	_ _e	_r_de	_r_me
p	o	_ _pe	_ _le	_ _st
p	u	_r_ne	_ _re	_ _ke

"He (<u>the king</u>) commanded (<u>sent</u>)… the soldiers to… throw them (<u>the friends</u>) <u>into</u> <u>the</u> furnace of blazing <u>fire</u>… He (<u>God</u>) <u>sent</u> <u>His</u> <u>angel</u> <u>and</u> rescued (<u>saved</u>) His servants (the friends) <u>who</u> trusted (<u>loved</u>) <u>Him</u>." Daniel 3:20,28 HCSB

Lesson 11 | Daniel in the Lions' Den

Daniel

How are you?	
11	

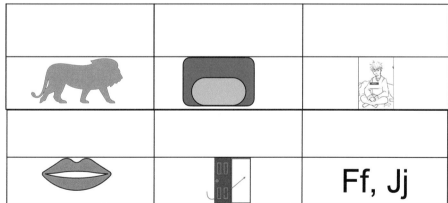

		Ff, Jj

NOUNS: Person, Place, Thing (Who? Or What?)

f-	f-	j-	j-

94

1. The _____ _____ is _____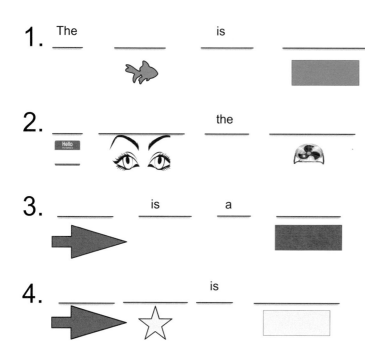

2. _____ _____ the _____

3. _____ _____ is a _____ _____

4. _____ _____ is _____

5. _____ _____ the _____ 5 _____ to _____

6. The _____ _____ _____ the _____

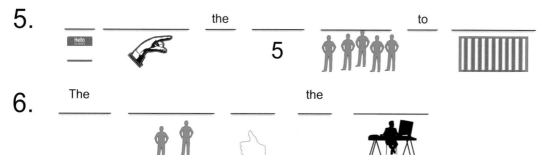

7. _____ _____ on _____
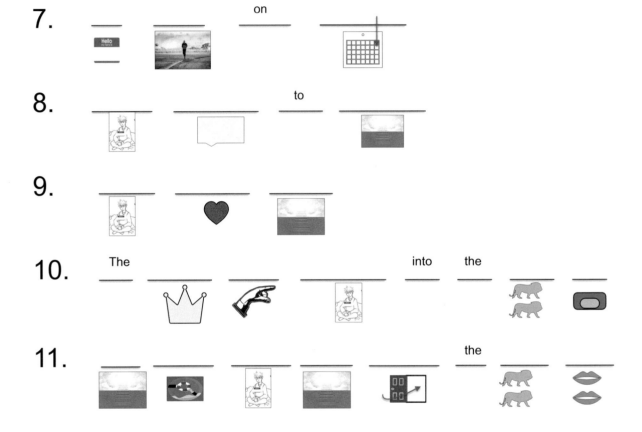

8. _____ _____ to _____

9. _____ _____ _____

10. The _____ _____ _____ _____ into the _____ _____

11. _____ _____ _____ _____ _____ the _____ _____

1
2
3
4
5
6
7
8
9
10
11
12

f	a	_ _n	_ _t	_ _st
f	e	_ _ll	_ _d	_ _lt
f	i	_ _sh	_ _t	_ _x
f	o	_ _x	_ _b	_ _g
f	u	_ _n	_ _r	_ _ss

f	a	_ _il	_ _te	_ _me
f	e	_ _et	_ _al	_ _e
f	i	_ _le	_ _le	_ _ght
f	o	_ _am	_ _ld	_l_at
f	u	_l_te	_ _se	_l_ke

j	a	_ _m	_ _x	_ _b
j	e	_ _t	_ _lly	_ _w
j	i	_ _g	_ _ff	(e)_ _nks
j	o	_ _b	_ _g	_ _ck
j	u	_ _mp	_ _st	_ _g

j	a	_ _il	_ _de	_ _mes
j	e	_ _sus	_ _ans	_ _ep
j	i	_ _ve		
j	o	_ _ke	_ _in	_ _int
j	u	_ _ne	_ _ly(i)	_ _ke

"So the <u>king</u> gave the order, and they brought <u>Daniel</u> and <u>threw</u> him <u>into</u> <u>the</u> <u>lions'</u> <u>den</u>." Daniel 6:16 HCSB

"'My <u>God</u> <u>sent</u> <u>His angel</u> <u>and</u> <u>shut</u> <u>the lions'</u> <u>mouths</u>...'" Daniel 6:22

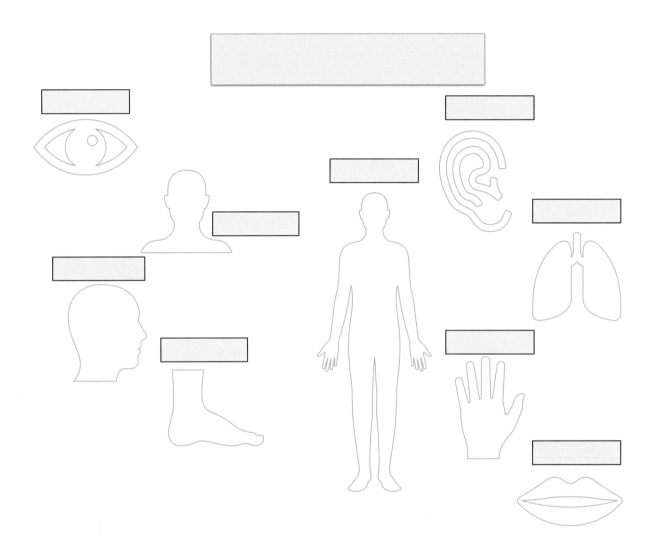

Lesson 12 Jonah and the Big Fish

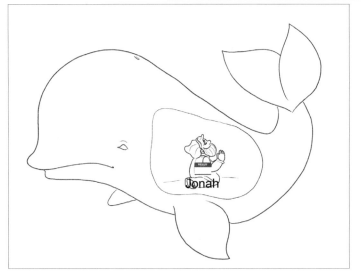

I'm fine. Thank you.

11
12

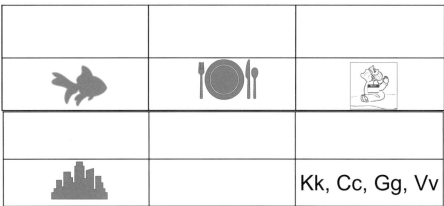

		Kk, Cc, Gg, Vv

NOUNS: Person, Place, Thing (Who? Or What?)

k-	k-	c-	c-

NOUNS: Person, Place, Thing (Who? Or What?)

g-	g-	v-	v-

g-   g-   v-   v-

104

1. The _____ _____ is _____

2. The _____ _____ is _____

3. _____ _____ is _____ _____

4. _____ _____ is _____

5. _____ _____ to _____

6. _____ _____ _____

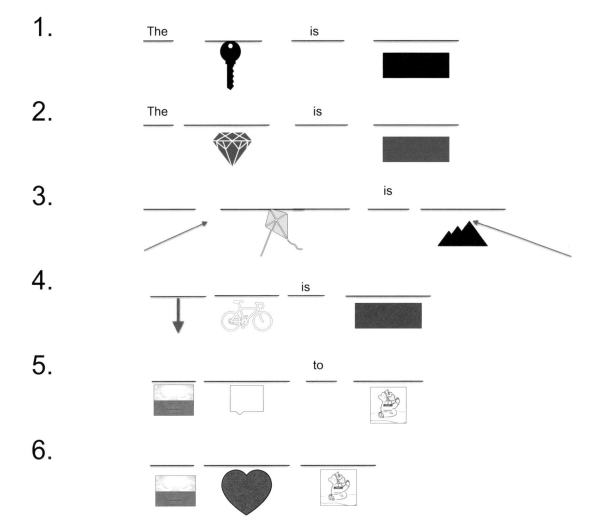

7. 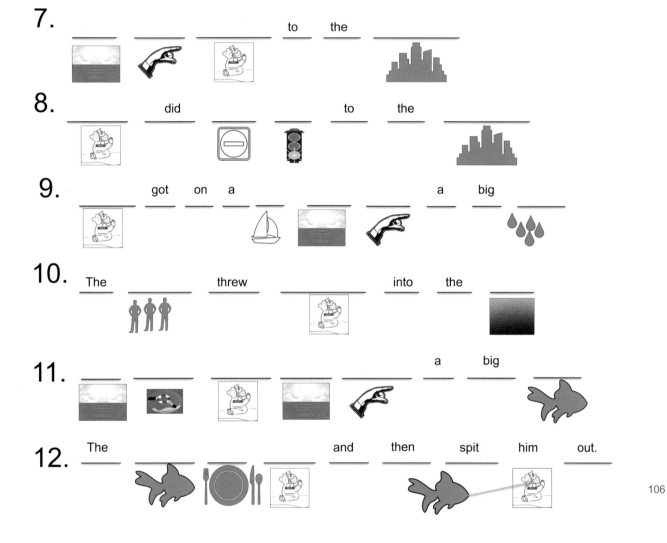 _____ _____ _____ to the _____

8. _____ did _____ _____ to the _____

9. _____ got on a _____ _____ _____ a big _____

10. The _____ threw _____ into the _____

11. _____ _____ _____ _____ _____ a big _____

12. The _____ _____ and then _____ spit him out.

1	
2	
3	
4	
5	
6	
7	
8	
9	
10	
11	
12	

k	a	_ _nsas	par_ _	Alas_ _
k	e	_ _d	_ _g	_ _pt
k	i	_ _ck	s_ _t	_ _ss
k	o	s_ _rt	coo_ _ff	kic_ _ff
k	u	s_ _ll	s_ _nk	bac_ _p

k	a	_ _ngaroo	o_ _y	_ _le
k	e	_ _y	_ _ep	_ n_el
k	i	_ _te	_ _nd	-
k	o	_ _ala	wa_ _	gecko
k	u	_ _dos	hai_ _	-

c	a	_ _me	_ _se	_ _ve
c	e	_ _de	_ _dar	s_ _ne
c	i	_ _te	_ _der	exer_ _se
c	o	_ _ke	_ _de	_ _ast
c	u	_ _te	_ _e	_ _re

c	a	_ _n	_ _b	_ _r
c	e	_ _real	_ _nt	_ _lebrate
c	i	a_ _d	_ _nema	_ _vil
c	o	_ _me	_ _lor	_ _n
c	u	_ _b	_ _t	_ _d

g	a	_ _ther	_ _mble	_ _p
g	e	_ _t	_ _ntle	_u_st
g	i	_ _affe	_ _ggle	_ _rl
g	o	_ _t	_ _d	_ _b
g	u	_ _m	_ _t	_ _lf

g	a	_ _te	_ _le	_ _ve
g	e	_l_am	_ _ar	_l_e
g	i	_l_de	_u_de	_r_nd
g	o	_l_w	_l_be	_ _re
g	u	_l_e	_l_te	ar_ _e

v	a	_ _t	_ _cuum	_ _ult
v	e	_ _t	_ _nt	_ _x
v	i	_ _sion	ci_ _l	_ _ _ _d
v	o	_ _lume	fa_ _r	_ _mit
v	u	_ _lture	-	-

v	a	_ _il	_ _in	_ _por
v	e	_ _al	_ _to	-
v	i	_ _olet	di_ _de	_ _le
v	o	_ _te	_ _lt	_ _cabulary
v	u	-	-	-

e

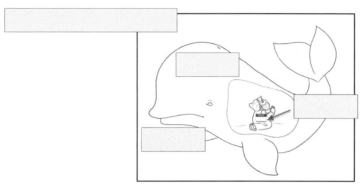

"And the <u>Lord (God)</u> <u>appointed (sent)</u> <u>a</u> great <u>fish</u> to <u>swallow (ate)</u> Jonah…

"Then the <u>Lord (God)</u> <u>commanded (spoke to)</u> <u>the fish</u>, and it <u>vomited (spit)</u> <u>Jonah out.</u>" Jonah 2:10

Lesson 13   Christmas - Jesus Came

	Merry Christmas
11	
12	
13	

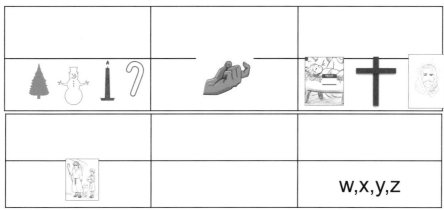

w,x,y,z

NOUNS: Person, Place, Thing (Who? Or What?)			
w	**x**	**y**	**z**

		2021	

	6		

1. _____ _____ the _____ _____

2. The _____ is _____

3. The _____ _____ the _____ _____

4. _____ _____ the _____ _____ _____

5. _____ _____ _____ _____

6. The _____ _____ to the _____ _____

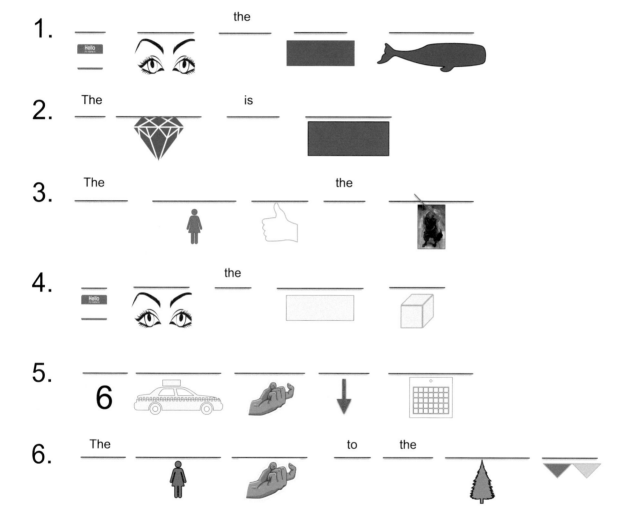

7. The _____ 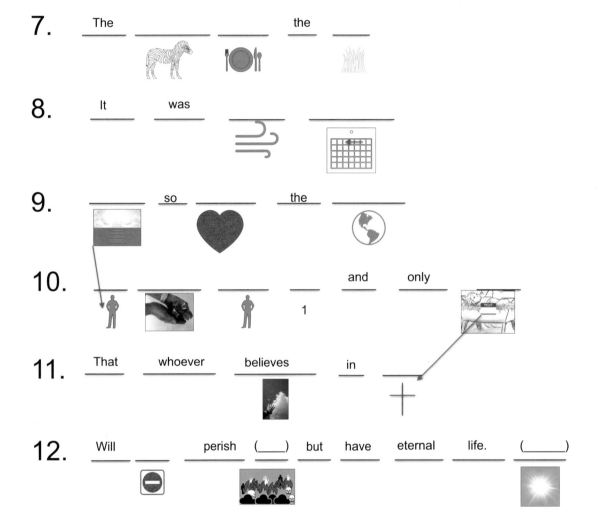 _____ the _____

8. It was _____ _____

9. _____ so _____ the _____

10. _____ _____ _____ _____ and only _____

11. That whoever believes in _____

12. Will _____ perish (_____) but have eternal life. (_____)

1	
2	
3	
4	
5	
6	
7	
8	
9	
10	
11	
12	

w	a	_ _ter	_ _g	_ _rm
w	e	_ _st	_ _d	_ _nt
w	i	_ _g	_ _n	_ _sh
w	o	_ _lf	_ _rk	_ _n
w	u	s_ _ng	-	-

w	a	_h_le	_ _de	_ _ke
w	e	_ _ed	_ _ek	_ _
w	i	_h_te	_ _nd	_ _de
w	o	_ _ke	-	-
w	u	-	-	-

a	x	_ _	t_ _i(e)	f_ _
e	x	T_ _as	M_ _ico	s_ _
i	x	s_ _	m_ _	f_ _
o	x	_ _	f_ _	b_ _
u	x	t_ _	del_ _e	-

y	a	_ _k	_ _m	_'_all
y	e	_ _s	_ _llow	_ _sterday
y	i	_ _p	-	-
y	o	_ _nder	ma_ _r	cra_ _n
y	u	_ _ck	_ _m	-

y	a	_ _y	-	-
y	e	_ _ar	y_ _st	-
y	i	_ _kes	-	-
y	o	_ _lk	_ _ke	_ _-_ _
y	u	_ _le	_o_	_ _ca

z	a	_ _g	_ _p	pizza
z	e	_ _st	do_ _n	fro_ _n
z	i	_ _p	_ _lch	_ _g
z	o	_ _mbie	-	-
z	u	-	-	-

z	a	-	-	-
z	e	_ _ro	_ _bra	-
z	i	-	-	-
z	o	_ _ne	-	-
z	u	-	-	-

"For <u>God</u> so <u>loved</u> <u>the</u> <u>world</u> that He(<u>God</u>) <u>gave</u> <u>His</u> only begotten <u>Son</u>, that <u>whoever</u> <u>believes</u> in Him(<u>Jesus</u>) <u>will</u> <u>not</u> perish(<u>go to hell</u>), but have eternal life(<u>be saved to go to Heaven</u>)." John 3:16 NASB

121

CONGRATULATIONS

Level 1 - Completed
Level 2
Level 3
Level 4
Level 5

Go to www.TexasBibleEnglish.com

for level 2 books and videos.

Review Questions

Lesson 8:

1. Who did David kill?

2. What did David use to kill the giant?

3. Who helped David kill the giant?

Lesson 9:

1. What did King Solomon bulid?

2. Who told King Solomon to build the temple?

Review Questions

Lesson 10:

1. Who sent the friends into the fire?

2. Who did God send to help the friends?

3. Who are your friends?

Lesson 11:

1. Where did the bad king send Daniel?

2. Who did God send to help Daniel?

3. Does God help you?

Review Questions

Lesson 12:

1. What ate Jonah?

2. What did God tell the big fish to do?

Lesson 13:

1. Why did God send His Son, Jesus?

2. Do you believe in Jesus and trust Him to save you?

3. Do you want to give your life to Jesus and live for Him?

Made in the USA
Columbia, SC
18 August 2024

40673445R00071